Sept 2018

AIR MASSES AND FRONTS

MARIEL BARD

PowerKiDS
press.

NEW YORK

Published in 2019 by The Rosen Publishing Group, Inc.
29 East 21st Street, New York, NY 10010

Editor: Hannah Fields
Cover Design: Michael Flynn
Interior Layout: Reann Nye

Photo Credits: Cover Minerva Studio/Shutterstock.com; p. 5 Patty Chan/Shutterstock.com; p. 6 Drew Angerer/Getty Images News/Getty Images; p. 7 simonkr/E+/Getty Images; p. 9 Himanshu Saraf/Shutterstock.com; p. 10 Anton Gvozdikov/Shutterstock.com; p. 11 https://commons.wikimedia.org/wiki/File:Air_masses.svg; p. 13 Courtesy of the NOAA; pp. 14, 19 Rainer Lesniewski/Shutterstock.com; p. 15 Jeff Gammons StormVisuals/Shutterstock.com; pp. 17, 21 Courtesy of the Library of Congress; p. 18 Astrid Gast/Shutterstock.com; p. 22 Nemeziya/Shutterstock.com.

Cataloging-in-Publication Data

Names: Bard, Mariel.
Title: Air masses and fronts / Mariel Bard.
Description: New York : PowerKids Press, 2019. | Series: Spotlight on weather and natural disasters | Includes glossary and index.
Identifiers: LCCN ISBN 9781508168683 (pbk.) | ISBN 9781508168669 (library bound) | ISBN 9781508168690 (6 pack)
Subjects: LCSH: Air masses--Juvenile literature. | Fronts (Meteorology)--Juvenile literature.
Classification: LCC QC880.4.A5 B36 2019 | DDC 551.55'12--dc23

Manufactured in the United States of America

CPSIA Compliance Information: Batch #CS18PK For further information contact Rosen Publishing, New York, New York at 1-800-237-9932.

CONTENTS

CHAPTER ONE

WEATHER ON EARTH

Weather is all around us and affects everyone on the planet. When it's cold and snowy, we put on our warm jackets. When it's rainy, we get out our umbrellas. The weather changes all the time, and it's important that we're prepared!

All the weather we experience happens because of air masses, which are like giant bubbles of air moving around the troposphere. The troposphere is the bottom layer of Earth's atmosphere. This layer extends from Earth's sea level to roughly 6.2 miles (10 km) into the sky. The different surfaces and temperatures on our planet affect the air contained within the troposphere. Air masses formed over warm water are different from air masses formed over cold, dry land. The boundary between two air masses is called a front, and when two air masses meet, the weather changes.

If you've ever looked out the window while on a large passenger airplane, you might have noticed a layer of clouds. You're actually looking down at the troposphere, where all our weather happens!

CHAPTER TWO

STUDYING EARTH'S ATMOSPHERE

Meteorology is the study of Earth's atmosphere and its effect on weather. The scientists who work in this field are called meteorologists. They want to know how and why certain weather events happen so they can better **predict** them.

Changes in weather occur when different air masses meet. So, tracking where air masses form,

Some meteorologists work at television stations and give weather reports during the news, while others work at **research** centers trying to improve weather predictions.

what features they have, and how they interact helps meteorologists figure out what the weather will be like.

Air masses form when air in the atmosphere sits above one large spot with uniform temperature and **humidity**. There must be little wind to push it away, so it picks up the features of the surface below. Air masses can spread over hundreds or even thousands of miles, and they can reach from Earth's surface to the top of the troposphere.

CHAPTER THREE

WHAT MAKES AN AIR MASS?

The features of an air mass are determined by the surface of Earth beneath it, which is called a source region. There are four main types of air masses based on these regions: Arctic, polar, **tropical**, and equatorial.

Arctic air masses are very cold and originate in the world's Arctic and Antarctic regions (around the North and South Poles). Polar air masses are not as cold as Arctic ones, and they form over areas of high latitude, such as much of Canada. Tropical air masses are warmer and found in low-latitude regions, such as the Caribbean Sea. Equatorial air masses are also warm, but they form along the equator.

The humidity of an air mass depends on the humidity of the surface below. If an air mass forms over water, it is classified as **maritime** and contains more moisture. If it forms over land, it's **continental** and drier.

Polar bears like this one are pros at living in cold weather. But when scientists warn of an Arctic air mass heading toward warmer areas, we humans need to bundle up!

CHAPTER FOUR

LABELING AIR MASSES

In order to keep track of air masses, Swedish meteorologist Tor Bergeron came up with a system to label them. It's called the Bergeron **classification** system, and it uses letters of the alphabet to label each feature an air mass might have.

To label air masses based on the amount of moisture they have, meteorologists use a lowercase "m" for maritime air masses and a lowercase "c" for continental. To show the source region of an air mass, they use an uppercase "A" for Arctic, a "P" for polar, a "T" for tropical,

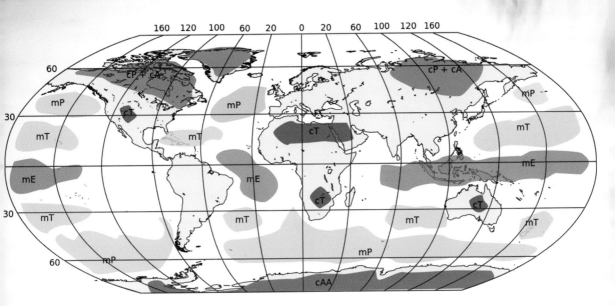

and an "E" for equatorial. There are also a few other types. Finally, a "w" says the air mass is warmer than the ground below it, and a "k" says it's colder.

By combining these letters, we label the features of air masses very easily. For example, "mTw" means that we have a maritime air mass from the tropics that's warmer than the surface below it.

CHAPTER FIVE

WHEN AIR MASSES MEET: FRONTS

There are two main types of fronts: cold fronts and warm fronts. A cold front is where a cold air mass replaces a warm air mass. A warm front is where a warm air mass replaces a cold air mass. Most of the weather events we experience happen at these fronts, so meteorologists keep track of them to try to predict when and where bad weather will happen.

You might be wondering why cold and warm air masses don't just mix, like how warm and cold water mix evenly when you pour one into the other. While air masses might mix a little bit along the edges, they can't combine completely. Air masses have different temperatures and densities. Density is how much mass there is per volume of air. Warm air rises, while cold air sinks.

Sometimes a front looks like a solid wall of clouds. There's often some kind of **precipitation**, such as rain or snow, at a front.

CHAPTER SIX

COLD FRONTS

Have you ever gone to school on a warm day but, by the time you left for home, it was cold and windy? A cold front moving through your area likely caused this.

When a cold air mass meets a warm air mass, the colder air may **displace** the warmer air, pushing it higher into the atmosphere. This moving edge of the cold air mass is the cold front. At Earth's surface, we often feel the quick drop in temperature as the colder air moves in. If the displaced warm air has enough moisture in it,

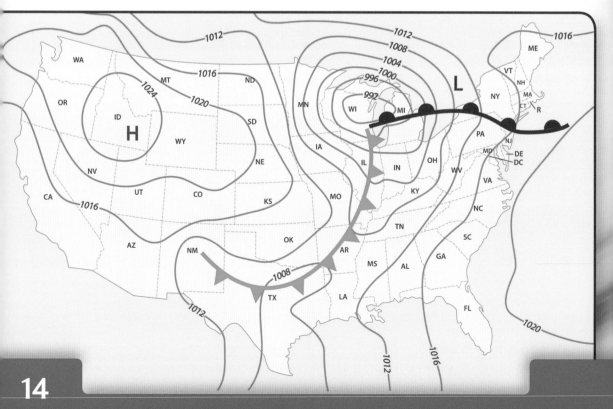

Severe weather is often a result of cold air masses pushing warm air masses up and out. When this happens, we can get strange-looking clouds that are full of moisture from the displaced warm air mass. What follows are thunderstorms with lightning, and lots of rain.

rain showers and sometimes thunderstorms may happen. This is because, as the warm air rises into the atmosphere, it cools off and the water vapor within **condenses**, turning into rain.

On a weather map, a blue line represents a cold front. There are triangles pointing in the direction the cold air mass is moving.

CHAPTER SEVEN

WARM FRONTS

When a warm air mass follows a retreating cold air mass, the leading edge of the warm air mass is a warm front. As a cold air mass leaves an area, a warm air mass can follow behind, also bringing increased humidity.

The warm air mass chases the back end of the cold air mass, which forces the warm, moist air up higher into the atmosphere. The air cools, and the water vapor condenses and falls back to Earth as rain. Bands of precipitation that come from warm fronts are usually broader and more uniform than bands of precipitation caused by cold fronts, without strong storms. It might seem strange, but during cold winter months, a warm front can lead to snow showers or even cause a blizzard due to all the moisture it carries!

On a weather map, a red line represents a warm front. Semicircles point in the direction the warm air mass is moving.

As a warm air mass approaches a cold air mass, its warm, moist air rises into the atmosphere over the chillier air of the cold air mass. This often creates a band of rain showers.

CHAPTER EIGHT

OTHER TYPES OF FRONTS

Cold and warm fronts are not the only types of fronts. In fact, air masses can meet and create new types of fronts. If one air mass can't displace the other, we get a stationary front. This means the boundary between the competing warm and cold air masses stays fairly consistent, with very little movement. Depending on the

This map shows a number of fronts as they move across Europe. Red lines with semicircles mean warm fronts, blue lines with triangles mean cold fronts, and pink lines with semicircles and triangles mean occluded fronts.

moisture content of the two fronts, either no rain will fall or quite a lot can. This can cause problems such as flooding because, if the front isn't moving, a lot of rain may fall in one area.

Because cold fronts tend to move a bit faster than warm ones, a cold front can catch up to a warm front to create an **occluded** front. This is the rarest and most **complex** type of front, but the resulting weather is usually similar to that caused by cold fronts.

CHAPTER NINE

PREDICTING THE WEATHER

Scientists try to predict the weather based on what they know about air masses and fronts and how they interact. Learning about air masses—such as source region, speed, temperature, and moisture content—can help meteorologists make guesses about upcoming weather.

Meteorologists have to combine their knowledge of atmospheric science with the live data they receive from **satellites**, weather stations, and **radar** images. After going through all this information, meteorologists create models using advanced computer programs. These models are digital representations of weather that can be studied and used to predict real weather.

Once all the data has been studied, meteorologists present their final predictions as a **forecast** that you can see during the weather report on television! However, the weather can change unexpectedly, so it's hard to have a forecast be 100 percent correct.

METEOROLOGICAL OBSERVATIONS,

Made at SPRINGMILL, 13 miles NNW. of PHILADELPHIA, 40° 9′ N.   Month of JANUARY, 1787.

D. of the month	THERMOMETER of FARENHEIT mean degree D. $\frac{1}{10}$		THERMOMETER de REAUMUR degrés moyens D. $\frac{1}{10}$		BAROMET. mean height in. pts. $\frac{1}{10}$			PREVAILING WIND	of aur. boreal	of rain	of thunder	of snow	of tempest	WATER of RAIN and SNOW, in. pts. $\frac{1}{10}$		WEATHER.
1	47	7	6	8	30	8		still								Fog, thick, humidity, warm.
2	44	2	5	5	29	11		still								Idem, after sund.
3	42		4	5	29	8	4	idem	1					14		Idem, after rain.
4	45	4	6		29	5	2	idem	1					5		Idem.
5	43	8	5	2	29	5	5	variable								Brisk wind, fair.
6	34	7	1	2	30			W N W								Fine.
7	34	2	1		30	1	5	S S E								Overcast.
8	36	4	2		29	10	7	still								Idem.
9	30		7	0	29	7	3	N E	1					13		Snow and rain.
10	29		3		29	5	8	still								Clouds and overcast, thaw.
11	28		1	7 0	29	6	7	idem								Clouds and fair.
12	23		4		29	8	8 0	W N W								Fair and clouds, brisk wind.
13	26	7	2	3	30	1	8	N W								Clouds and fair.
14	35	9	1	7	29	10	8	variable								Fair.
15	47		6	7	29	5	4	S W								Overcast, thaw.
16	38	1	2	7	29	6		idem								Fair.
17	36		1	8	29	3	7	W								Very fair, brisk wind.
18	35		1	5	29	7		W								Idem, brisk wind.
19	21		4	8 0	30	1	7	variable								Fair, overcast.
20	35	4	2	5	29	8	3	still				1			1	Overcast, small snow.
21	35	4	2	5	29	9	9	E N E	1	1				4		Overcast, rain, thunderstorm.
22	34	2	1		30	1	7	idem	1					6	3	Rain.
23	29	6	1	0	30	2		idem	1					6	2	Rain.
24	43	4	5		29	8	9	W		1					8	Snow, fog, rain.
25	32	7	3		30		9	still	1						2	Fog and rain.
26	35	4	2	5	29	9	8	idem							1	Inconstant.
27	36	4	2		29	11		W		1				10	13	Snow, rain.
28	27	4	2	0	30	3		W								Fine.
29	25	1	3	0	29	9		variable		1				4	8	Snow.
30	35	4	2	5	29	7		still								Fine.
31	32			0	29	11	9	still								Fine.

RESULT

19th greatest D. of cold. 16 3	le 19. D. du plus gr. froid. 7 0	the 28. greatest elevation 30 3 8					
1st greatest D. of heat. 56 8	le 1. plus G.D. de chaud. 11	the 4th least elevation. 29 3 5	Changeable & still.	7 1 4	3 10 10		Fair, still, cold, and snow.
Variation 40 5	Variation 18	Variation 1 3					
Temperature 35	Temperature 14	mean elevation 29 9 10					

226628
15

Before computers were invented, scientists recorded the weather by hand. This record dates back to 1787 and includes the temperature, pressure, winds, precipitation, and overall weather. Humans have been working to understand and predict the weather for centuries!

CHAPTER TEN

IT'S ALL IN THE AIR

Recognizing all the types of air masses and fronts created in Earth's atmosphere lets us prepare for changes in our weather. When we label them based on their features, we can quickly know their possible impacts. And studying and tracking fronts helps us see where bad weather is likely to occur.

The study of meteorology is always improving, and the computer models meteorologists use can provide more information. This means we may soon be able to give plenty of warning to people in areas that might be hit by severe weather, such as hurricanes, blizzards, and tornadoes, so they can prepare and stay safe.

Scientists also work hard to understand weather and how and why it changes to tell us what to expect so that we can plan our days. From beautiful blue skies to thunderstorms and rain, the weather we experience is all driven by air masses and their fronts.

GLOSSARY

classification (clah-suh-fuh-KAY-shuhn) Arrangement of something into groups based on certain guidelines.

complex (kahm-PLEHKS) Not easy to understand or explain, having many parts.

condense (con-DEHNS) To lose heat and change from a gas into a liquid.

continental (kahn-tuh-NEN-tahl) Having to do with the mainland part of a country.

displace (dis-PLAYS) To take something else's place or position.

forecast (FOR-kast) A prediction of future conditions. Also, to predict future conditions based on data.

humidity (huu-MIH-duh-tee) The amount of moisture in the air.

maritime (MAR-uh-time) Having to do with the seas.

occlude (uh-CLOOD) In meteorology, when a cold front catches up to and merges with a warm front, forming an occluded front.

precipitation (pruh-sih-puh-TAY-shuhn) Water that falls to the ground as hail, mist, rain, sleet, or snow.

predict (pri-DIHCT) To guess what will happen in the future based on facts or knowledge.

radar (RAY-dahr) A machine that uses radio waves to locate and identify objects.

research (REE-suhrch) Careful study of something.

satellite (SAA-tuh-lyt) A spacecraft placed in orbit around Earth, a moon, or a planet to collect information or for communication.

tropical (TRAH-puh-kul) Warm and wet, having to do with the tropics.

INDEX

PRIMARY SOURCE LIST

Page 13
Shelf cloud. Photograph. Taken by Sean Waugh. May 7, 2008. NOAA's National Severe Storms Laboratory (NSSL) Collection.

Page 17
Storm clouds. Photograph. Taken by Carol M. Highsmith. October 2, 2015. Library of Congress, Prints and Photographs Division.

Page 21
Meteorological observations, made at Springmill, 13 miles NNW of Philadelphia. Photograph. January 1787. Library of Congress.

WEBSITES

Due to the changing nature of Internet links, PowerKids Press has developed an online list of websites related to the subject of this book. This site is updated regularly. Please use this link to access the list: www.powerkidslinks.com/swnd/airmf